The Zen
of
Haiku

1000 TINY POEMS

Jay Verney

ZKB

Zen Kettle Books | Brisbane, Australia

Zen Kettle Books
Contact: dottyink@yahoo.com

Publisher's Note: This is a work of poetry. Names, characters, places, and incidents are a product of the authors' imaginations. Locales and public names are sometimes used for atmospheric purposes. Any resemblance to actual people, living or dead, or to businesses, companies, events, institutions, or locales is completely coincidental.

Book Cover Design: © Jay Verney & Lorrie Lawler

ISBN 978-0-9945470-7-1

A catalogue record for this
book is available from the
NATIONAL LIBRARY OF AUSTRALIA
National Library of Australia

For Lorrie, of course

To see a World in a Grain of Sand,
And a Heaven in a Wild Flower,
Hold Infinity in the palm of your hand,
And Eternity in an hour

WILLIAM BLAKE

\# 1
Today
forty cockatoos
in flying conversation

#2
Black tea and
toast
A little butter

#3
Red-jammy scones
halved
Hot – there's steam

#4
Boiling rice
steaming starch
a silky swallow

#5
Do you remember
falling
asleep

#6
Large dry leaf
scraping bitumen:
an injured bird

#7
Watching insects
cluster and circle
in focused chaos

#8
Crumpling cellophane
the crackle and burn of it
especially red

#9
First mouthful of beer
always
better than the rest

#10
Olive oil
fried onions and garlic
tomatoes toast

#11
On the top step
a white cat
no collar

#12
White onions
peeling layers
appealing to themselves

\# 13
Small brown
oval temptress
egg

#14
Dive-bombing myna
beak-snap
no blood, yet

#15
Magpies singing
or laughing
either one is love

#16
Blankets sun dry
winter almost done
another wash in it

#17
Swaying frond
dancing legless
with windy rhythm

#18
The spider moves
half an inch
taps its web

#19
Waiting with my cat
the warm
sun obliges

#20
Tea cup
on the step
half-full half-hot

#21
Clouds
slip-sliding on
teflon blue

#22
Empty house
empty chairs
air full

#23
Chicken and beans
compromise
lunch

#24
Clothesline turning
squeaks a
symphony

#25
Ticking clocks
in every room
battery time

#26
Until a weight
is lifted
is it heavy?

#27
Parsnip soup
home made
vegie work

#28
Baguette
garlic butter
lunch in a stick

#29
Mushroom and onion
gravy drapes
itself on dinner

#30
Paperwork
layered
inky

#31
Empty box
its memory of
reward

#32
The drawing board
has no drawings
identity crisis?

#33
Silent piano
as the metronome
ticks on

34
Chili beef
heated discussion
cold beer

#35
Mountain fire
orange by night
black soot dawn

#36
Lawn mowing neighbour
cut grass scent
childhood dreaming

#37
Rain wait
dry grass
crackle

#38
Tea cooling
day warming
a meeting

#39
Work is art
art is work
Workers though

#40
Veranda sitting
strokes the
breath

#41
Drying clothes
line dancing
Ha! They twirl

#42
Egg and bacon
together
best friends

\# 43
Cold night
layers
including cat

#44
Rising moon
large extra yellow
extra large yellow

#45
Navy sky
turning black
night birds tuning up

#46
Wild rosemary
formerly tame
scenting freedom

#47
Strawberry glut
daily delight
strawberry gut

#48
Raisin toast
hot raisins melt
the butter coat

#49
White on blue
clouds strolling
backdrop steady

#50
Spring blows in
tail-coating winter
sleeve-rolling

#51
Boiled egg mashed
with mayonnaise
lettuce wrapped

#52
Cake crumbs
on a plate
finger pad pressing

#53
Onion sliced
with stinging
goodness

#54
Hot cupcakes
and
white-cold milk

#55
Rain dropping
hesitant at
first

#56
The rice
separates
grain by grain

#57
Heat wave
lowering blinds
shade

#58
Dogs passing
dogs barking
high low choir

#59
Wet mop
dry air
floor clean

#60
Taco mince
if I add
spice

#61
At the end
of the day
another

#62
At the end
of the page
turn

#63
At the end
of the line
a semi-colon

#64
At the end
of the rope
not guilty

#65
Heat waving
hello to my
thermometer

#66
Buy a new
pen and write
your leftovers

67
Today's leftovers
six dollars in change
a cat's whisker

#68
Half a roll
toasted
poached egg on top

#69
Hot oats
with cold milk
sugar sprinkle

#70
Christmas sausages
squeeze wrapped
mystery gifts

#71
Little poems
stringing words along
loops and lacework

#72
When you
butter toast listen
for the spread

#73
Closing a
gate-latch
soothing smoothing catch

#74
Mosquito drone near
the left ear
Summer hit

#75
Reaching for tea
my wristwatch
reminds me

#76
Sitting in a
different place
the room is new

#77
Three bracelets
one wrist
about right

#78
Rain plunging
down the coast the
monsoon sobbing

#79
The heat
unrelenting
stretching its roll

#80
For rain is
but the sky
sweating bullets

#81
Fried rice
never the same
twice

#82
Follow the breath
all the way
home

#83
Windy rainy night
homeless counting
seconds

#84
My cat's ears
pointy not
sharp

#85
Pen
Paper
Moment

#86
What's nice
is to sit
quietly

#87
To a desert
island
dessert

#88
To a dessert
island
Tea

#89
To a desert
island
public radio

#90
To a desert
island
steak salad beer

#91
To a desert
island
jazz

#92
To a desert
island
love and like

#93
When you fall
asleep
Are you lost?

#94
As you fall
asleep
Are you found?

#95
The bathroom mirror
my steamy reflection
Revealed

#96
The bathroom mirror
my steamy reflection
Concealed

#97
Today our stray cat
came and went
came and stayed

#98
When a stray
cat stays
Is she home?

#99
Enchiladas
taste better
on rainy days

#100
Listening for
individual rain
drops

#101
Full moon
Bright night
Light sleep

#102
Paperback hero
foxed with age
far more charming

#103
Lying awake to the
party drumbeat on
Saturday night

#105
Air cooling fast
Sudden storm
Close windows

#105
Sleeping next to
the night
an open window

#106
When your beloved
snores
A gentle rock

#107
A cat
climbing the gate
Latch rattle

#108
Too many ticks
of the late night
second hand

#109
Bats and possums
Mid-summer midnight
Mango munchies

#110
Fresh sheets
A warm body
Between

#111
My aging cat
occupies
the executive chair

#112
The washing
beneath a blue
sky's benevolence

#113
Seafood crepes
from my beloved's
holiday hands

#114
On the night air
Barbecue smoke, jasmine
Rum and coke

#115
Through the night air
musical notes
drift in packs

#116
From the night air
a settling
damp

#117
Early morning garden
crisper
than later

#118
Paw prints
on the veranda
Dewy grass

#119
Tiny lizards conquer
rising ant hills
their mini Jurassic

#120
Rustling leaves
the assurance
of wind

#121
Today
new tea
old longing

#122
In the darkness
flapping wings
Bat or bird?

#123
Winter thunderstorm
rolling through
a mild week

#124
Sunny day
A cat and her servant
warm

#125
Empty letterboxes
after the mail run
Excitement withdrawn

#126
Junk mail
fluttering between
shrub and fence

#127
The wind outside
noisy leaves
In here it's still

#128
Raining sky
Muddy yard
A cat's wet paw

#129
On a blue sky
seagulls
stick

#130
Car washed
sunlight
dripping

#131
Christmas dinner gravy
almost like Mum's
Not quite

#132
One garden tree
with bug-lunched leaves
Must be tasty

\# 133
Old cat
settling into
her sunken cushion

\# 134
Where the car
was washed
muddy tyre tracks

#135
A tiny lizard
surfing grass blades
after the mowing

#136
Hover fly
buzzing through
waits a while

#137
Hungover
Move slowly
Move slowly

#138
Sun-curtaining
cloud
shadows the ground

#139
Unmarked graves
my ancestors'
grassy memorials

#140
Walking the
cemetery with
springy gratitude

#141
Saturday afternoon
Chips and beer
Disaster movie

#142
Well-cooked rice
each grain
itself

#143
Friday late
karaoke
very loud

#144
Hot tea
Hot day
Hot flush

#145
Steam rises
from my cup
Tea's breath

#146
Sipping, inhaling
Tea's breath
My breath

#147
When dieting
avoid
the kitchen-linger

#148
Before dawn
birds
call time

#149
Are thoughts
the mind's
children?

#150
Waiting for the
kettle to boil
steaming

#151
Sipping warm tea
from a saucer
when I was two

#152
Collecting
the neighbour's mail
Bills like mine

#153
Saturday afternoon
News of a death
Another friend gone

#154
At the service
Everyone older
Grass growing

#155
In the chapel
Musical break
Joy notes the sad air

#156
Memorial plaques
Names set and solid
Ours free

#157
After the service
Lotion on my hands
Rubbing life in

#158
My cat
at the vet
Our house alone

#159
At sunset
black crows tattoo
the full moon

#160
Twilight arriving
Sea breeze rising
Day tripping over

#161
The beach
Low tide
Spare sand

#162
On the beach
a dog
wave-stepping

#163
Our old cat
sleeping forever
loved

#164 – *Farewell Suite: 1*
The first death
the physical
Last breath

#165 – *Farewell Suite: 2*
The second death
the burial
Last light

#166 – *Farewell Suite: 3*
The final death
the memory
Last trace

#167
Tea colour
between
syrup and honey

#168
Is onion juice
an onion's
tears?

#169
Fried garlic
crunchy brown
Tiny meal

#170
Bruised basil
Greenly darkening
Hey pesto!

#171
Mothers shopping
Infants yelling
Babel market

#172
Old jeans
the comfort
of last century

#173
The first step
and another
one more one more

#174
Every step
the first if
there's only now

#175
The last step
always
a first

#176
Boil water
Spoon leaves
Brew tea – draw – sip

#177
Between steps
a sole
air cooled

#178
Between steps
a sole shadow
grounding

#179
Passing train
at midnight
For which day?

#180
A shower
approaching
paints the street

#181
Possums on the roof
pitching seeds at
tinny midnight

#182
Buzz, bark, screech,
cough, flap, tick
Midnight LP

#183
The kittens
we'll adopt
to be conceived

#184
Mowing in the rain
Green scents
and nonsense

#185
New editing job
Many words to
few

#186
New editing job
Many words
Too few

#187
Visiting black cat
asleep on our
welcome mat

#188
Stacking books
another and more
reading between spines

#189
When you wake
is your dream
with you?

#190
One dog barks
The choir responds
One dog barks

#191
Complaining crows
at midnight
Black feathers blacker

#192
The over the road
cat within
coaxing distance

#193
Breakfast oats
for dinner
A flexible chef

#194
Bed of lettuce
instead of rice
Weightless colour

#195
Rainy night
White noise
in the dark

#196
Rainy morning
The light
oversleeping

#197
Showers easing
Drip feeding
dawn

#198
Summer's
boastful grass
Its greeniness

#199
Drinking water
after the heat
A cool slide

#200
Autumn sky
far too blue
Summer's wagging tail

#201
Folding laundry
it seems
even cleaner

#202
In the absence
of cake
its crumby presence

#203
After life
the psychic's
first thought?

#204
Cupcake birthday
icing the first
year's play

#205
Leaving earliness
to itself
on Sunday

#206
When honey
soaks in
pursue it spoonfully

#207
Shovelling a
bark-chip mountain
The garden's Everest

#208
School reunion
up north
Time and miles away

#209
Surprise
Saturday shower
Even the cat sprinkled

#210
Too many
cups of tea?
Impossible

#211
Syrup-sticky
knife handle
To lick or not to lick

#212
A Sharpie
waiting to write
with inky intentions

#213
Crime scene tape
stretching
its authority

#214
Every day
Dawn Noon Dusk
Birth Life Death

#215
The moon halves
the sun rises
washing dries

#216
So windy
our shadows
rising

#217
Winter freeze
in the tropics
half-hearted

#218
New kittens
Old scratching post
Ancestral home

#219
One day
Three lines
Momentary memoir

#220
One day
Short lines
Poem

#221
One day
long lines
Short story

#222
One day
many lines
Novel beginning

#223
The sun
behind me
has my back

#224
Shadow ahead
my own
Darkness leaving

#225
Beside me
a shadow strolls
Fingers stretching

#226
Coaxing
lavender my
hands fragrant

#227
Picking
rosemary
lamb roast nearer

#228
Returning library
books walking
home alone

#229
On the vacant
lot four galahs
calling it home

#230
Peeling mandarins
Sticky seedy sweet
afternoon tea

#231
Fluttering leaves
ahead
A wind picks up

#232
Rising sun
in my eyes
Too early walk

#233
Rising sun
in my eyes
Late as usual

#234
Rock wall
leaning against
gravity's game

#235
Roots like
worms make
for the gutter

#236
Chicken
on the loose
Feathers uncooped

#237
High-rise street
Low-rise steps
harder today

#238
Freshly dropped
rain rolling
and flat

#239
Waiting wheelbarrow
Same shovel
Different dirt

#240
Captured leaves
waiting on their
windy saviour

#241
Rolls of junk
mail scoping out
my wallet

#242
White cockatoo
Grubby green grass
snacks

#243
Short trees
entallen some
passersby

#244
Old cat
big yard
long walks

#245
Young cat
big yard
feather scatter

#246
Empty playground
catching
its breath

#247
On the
fallen ladder a
conquering snail

#248
Specky red
chopper way up
Dragonfly

#249
Empty playground
lonely as a
shoe

#250
Banana leaves
waving
fruitlessly

#251
Pots of
carnations
colour cramming

#252
Cushiony grass
thick
with bare feet

#253
Dog walking man
hyphen
optional

#254
First of Spring
lemon-scented gum
an early starter

#255
Kittens inside
Stray cat outside
Window talk

#256
Line of cars
not a funeral
the night shift over

#257
Pavers stacked
for placement
A last aimless walk

#258
Smog or fog
Smoke and mist at
the wind's pleasure

#259
Mother walking
mobile talking
baby squawking

#260
God rays
through the clouds
Sun struggle

#261
Garden pots
tossed aside
like outgrown shoes

#262
Freshly planted
library garden
Book lovers' herbs

#263
Vacant lot
hosts
a weed party

#264
Personalised plates
as rolling
ego ads

#265
Veterans' garden
plaque by plaque
petal by petal

#266
Warm sun
Cold wind compete
on my skin

#267
Bookleaf pine
open
for browsing

#268
Bicycles on
roof racks
changing gears

#269
Hilltop
Breathless
Done

#270
One sock
Partner missing
Career imperilled

#271
In the beginning
was the tea
then toast

#272
Scallopy sky
heading for
the sun

#273
After breakfast
another cup
and scone dreaming

#274
Young cat
sunning herself
for moments

#275
Old cat
sunning herself
sunning herself

#276
Today's paper
folded and fresh
unused news

#277
Woman with a
cane conducting
each step

#278
Barky little dog
safely inside
Barkier

#279
Man up ahead
his paper read
news dead

#280
Shed snakeskin
at the door
the serpentine mafia

#281
In the park
a barbecue
Invitation only

#282
Hands on hips
deep breath walking
End run

#283
The corner shop
now a home
New product range

#284
Minutes to seconds
to moments to
poems

#285
Piano practice
on the air
Street music

#286
Butterfly tattoo
on a
weightlifter's arm

#287
On the
designated path
clean soles

#288
Left-over cable
hoarding
transmissions

#289
Untrodden path
Old soles
Stories shared

#290
A skip full
of disorderly
history

#291
Hosing Spring's
garden from
Winter's water tank

#292
Paw prints in
wet cement
Anonymous celebrity

#293
Jasmine blooming
Spring looming cats
indifferently grooming

#294
Tiny pink slipper
at the bus stop
Cold toes somewhere

#295
Walking faster
Looking
not seeing

#296
Monday morning
fog the
weekend's hangover

#297
On the street a
cracked Beatles' CD
not *Abbey Road*

#298
Gardenia then
jasmine one breath
to the next

#299
Moment by moment
living and dying
Each and both

#300
Empty lots
face each other
Birds settle

#301
One lawn chaos
Next door's neat
A precise common edge

#302
Swooping magpie
the strength
of feathers

#303
Shopping mall
billboard all
colour – that's it

#304
The corner home's yard
garden gnome central
issuing passports

#305
Dummy on
the road
Baby's or driver's?

#306
Butcher-bird singing
I'll pretend
it's for me

#307
Do beautiful
letterboxes
get better mail?

#308
Palm fronds above
shushing
their garden

#309
Pretty yellow flowers
cover the vacant lot
Weeds, apparently

#310
Dead crow's eyes
glittering
from elsewhere

#311
Dead crow's
feathers a
dustier black

#312
Tail-less lizard
in the bathroom
Wet pawprints fading

#313
Lost cat poster
lost
in the storm

#314
Old chair
sanded dusted varnished
Newish chair

#315 – *Cloud Suite: 1*
Out-walking
the rain clouds
Umbrella at home

#316 – *Cloud Suite: 2*
Out-walking
the rain clouds
Their western swoop

#317 – *Cloud Suite: 3*
Out-walking
the rain clouds
They scatter

#318 – *Cloud Suite: 4*
Out walking
A shower
Temporary T-shirt art

#319 – *Cloud Suite: 5*
Out
walking with rain
its spitting images

#320
Dry road
Wet car
Showers elsewhere

#321
'Kristina's' name
drying in concrete
A longer life?

#322
For rent for lease
for sale
Forsaken space

#323
Tiny garage beside
a small house
The people?

#324
Rushing through the
drops sunshine
over there

#325
Faster slower dripping
on the umbrella
Rainy rhythm

#326
Plane flaying
rain clouds
Invisibly mending themselves

#327
If your dead
call the shots
are you alive?

#328
Dead mother's words
spoken by another
Stronger or weaker?

#329
White cockatoo flying
against blue the
sharpest of constrasts

#330
In the city
football fireworks jets
We try sleep

#331
Swooping magpie
Hidden nest
Angry Mama

#332
Healthy weeds
around the garden
Fit for purpose

#333
Solar panels
darkly gathering
light

#334
Black and yellow
scooter makes a
beeline for work

#335
The flag flying
above flat-weed
Patriotic growth

#336
Zeros
and their roundiness
Complete

#337
What's with five?
Halfway to?
Halfway from?

#338
Flat rocks
on the beach
skippable

#339
Older and younger
shooting baskets – the
ball doesn't know

#340
A gaggle
of runners
breathing by

#341
Dad striding
Son skipping
Work and school

#342
Following
a butterfly can be
difficult

#343
Fallen leaves
Did they jump or
were they pushed?

#344
In the shallows
a tiny fish
Just as well

#345
Storm birds calling
a month early
What do they know?

#346
Neville's corner fence
leaning and falling
after Neville

#347
Leaf blowers
fight the
silent majority

#348
A Porsche 911 –
with spoiler – in
speed-bumped suburbia

#349
Parrots hustle
brunch at the
Bottlebrush Bar and Shrill

#350
Cloudless blue
Bird and plane
Jacaranda reaching

#351
No time like
the present
So like it

#352
No time but
the present
No buts

#353
Like the present
No buts
And then?

#354
House keys jingle
with each step
away from home

#355
Storm clouds
descending ink
drops in water

#356
Jasmine and cinnamon
Springing the season
Garden brunch

#357
Listening for poems
out walking
Sneaky syllables

#358
Walking on the
first hot day
Go earlier

#359
Summer walks
Sunscreen water shade
Stay home

#360
Smoke haze
Cooling breeze
waves it through

#361
Butterflies catch
each other's
flutterstream

#362
Orange peel
left for birds
Sunnily souring

#363
Repainting
an old desk
Hiding agendas

#364
Zen dog
contemplates
barkworthy walkers

#365
Insects small fish
frogs a shoe
Creek running

#366
Band practice
at the barracks
Piping hot day

#367
50/50 for rain
Open and shut
brolly case

#368
Mashed potato
Blue plate
Cumulo-lessening

#369
Step
Step Step
Step Step Step

#370
Waiting at work
the day's events
packed tight

#371
On half-moon nights
half the sky
asleep

#372
The shadiest tree
when the hour
is right

#373
Towels line dry
after the beach
Sand-sifting wind

#374
Rain mist
so wispy
it's dry

#375
Squawks and rustles
Falling seeds
Hide and peck parrots

#376
A gardenia
breath-take
at the corner

#377
Crushing a
bookleaf pine seed
Nana decades gone

#378
Thoughts ahead
of steps
Only mindful feet

#379
Stop-Slow-Go-
guy lunching
between speeds

#380
Wind-shake of
jacaranda leaves
Lavender spill

#381
Fallen leaves
Breezy playthings
Second lives, third, fourth

#382
Bird-impersonating
jet
Rigid acting style

#383
The value of
going away:
coming home

#384
Rain-heavy clouds
spring leaks
beyond repair

#385
Storm gusts rising
leaves go to
ground, eventually

#386
Old 'Beware of
the dog' sign
Old dog? No dog?

#387
Sunny day
after the gloomy
shadows shape up

#388
Hot still day
A single gust
Yearning begins

#389
Ham tomato
onion olives lettuce
Let us lunch

#390
Life wears you
You wear life
Perhaps you break even

#391
Clouds
like flung sheets
Unmade sky

#392
Sulphur-crested cockatoo
Big Name
nameless bird

#393
Rain-looming gloom
Beaksful of twigs
Crows' storm-shutters

#394
On the footpath
a pen, somewhere
a notebook yearns

#395
On the footpath
a pen, its
life's words done

#396
Straight path curves
round a gum tree
Respect deeply rooted

#397
Jasmine scent in
every summer street
Blooming marvellous

#398
Grass-clip spill
decorates the road
Accidental street art

#399
Sky drips play
hide and seek
in the clouds

#400
Summer grass rises
Banking inches
against the heat

#401
Walking the block an
unexpected car
Mortality as hatchback

#402
Returning a ball
over the fence
A barking thanks

#403
Weekend litter on
weekday footpath
Crossing party lines

#404
Dropped dead behind
the mower grass
untouched growing

#405
Teething keys dropped
from a pram
Locked gums somewhere

#406
After heavy rain
gardeners and birds digging
softness

#407
Cockatoo perched above
ground-lunching mates
Being the cockatoo*   *(a lookout)

#408   (after the Lindt café Sydney siege)
Early morning
Darkness and light
before dawn

#409   (after the Lindt café Sydney siege)
After the breaking
the breaking day
Light and flowers

#410
Summer's darkness
Sea breeze and heatwave
Syrupy midnight rollers

#411
Stepping up
the hill angling
for ease

#412
Waiting on a
cloudburst patience
drying up

#413
In darkness the
steaming kettle
looks cool

#414
Kittens play
for keeps
in seconds

#415
Your foot
in a shoe
The wiggle room

#416
Grass clippings
flung about
Hay for ants

#417
Clouds spitting
at me
No offence taken

#418
At the turning
of leaves another
season's books

#419
Election day winner
still votes away
Buy fudge

#420
The tree now
metres tall
And its birth height?

#421
A child's voice
in play
on the wind

#422
Short mat
Long cat
Stretching a friendship

#423
Perfumed passerby
carries a lavender
trail from home

#424
Grass grows audibly
with the monsoon
Sole-crooning blades

#425
Clouds like
popping corn
growing and rising

#426
Flowers leaning
one way
Solar politics

#427
Workers uniformed, fresh
and pressed, bejewelled,
enter Monday's stage

#428
Surprised by an
early morning moon
still hanging around

#429
Passing car
Passing voices
Mobile conversation

#430
Weeds arching across
the footpath low-slung
guard of honour

#431
Sunday cars coasting by
A long slow ocean
wave

#432
Half-moon hungover from
the night before
That glary sun

#433
Library book half-read
by the due date
Risk the fine?

#434
Arriving early with
departure in mind - so
disdained this place?

#435
That smell of
rain so like the
earth

#436
That smell of
rain invites
deep breaths

#437
Rattling bottles
next door late
the party's end

#438
Thunder nearby
and nearer
Kittens clustering

#439
On the breeze
perfume and smoke
Saturday night barbecue

#440
Green tree snake
silently watches
me watching it

#441
Lingering smoke stuck
to damp air
its taste sharpens

#442
Listening for birdsong
beyond the traffic
where birds listen

#443
Walking this morning
with a noiseless
half-minute – thanks

#444
The warming company of
silence but for
your own steps

#445
Dead fronds swaying
a farewell from
the skip's edge

#446 – *Brown Gravy Suite: 1*
Brown gravy on toast
Just that
Maybe parmesan shavings

#447 – *Brown Gravy Suite: 2*
Brown gravy on toast
Slide a fried
egg between

#448 – *Brown Gravy Suite: 3*
Brown gravy and
spuds – wedge-cut
salty, crunchy-creamy

#449 – *Brown Gravy Suite: 4*
Brown gravy and
roast chicken
Natural compatriots

#450 – *Brown Gravy Suite: 5*
Leftovers under brown gravy
Who knows the
difference?

#451 – *Brown Gravy Suite: 6*
Brown gravy with an
onion-y garlic-y inclination
Rosemary lamb roast

#452 – *Brown Gravy Suite: 7*
Brown gravy and
ice-cream? Depends
on the ice-cream

#453 – *Brown Gravy Suite: 8*
Brown gravy no recipe
one question:
Is it more-ish, then?

#454
Eager blades of
grass pointing out
the sky

#455
Dad's birthday
coming and going
without him

#456
Hat-lifting winds
camped at the
corner

#457
Steaming
Heatwave
Tea and Summer

#458
The tree snake coiling
a branch with
all the world's time

#459
Two cats, sisters,
sparring like ...
sisters

#460
Last night almost
a full moon toying
with edges and clouds

#461
Our local garden snake
rustling
between beds

#462
A free rainbow
with this morning's walk
And fairy mist garnish

#463
Simple dull rocks
glittering after rain
Sunshine's tricky polish

#464
Shadowy veranda, huge
sleek cat – oh wait,
pointy-eared dog

#465
Flushing perfection
absolutely draining
The plumber's visit

#466
Long planks sliding
Nail gun driving
New floor tango

#467
Moonlight falling
on yesterday's puddles
Today's reflections

#468
Tiny tent towns
White splashing green
Mushroom paddock

#469
The keys in my
pocket tinkling
high and sweet today

#470
Does everyone get to
stand on grass once –
and barefoot

#471
Leftover summer thunder
and lightning crash
autumn's opening night

#472
My cat chasing
her tail as though
it's her teasing sister's

#473
Long food
Short break
Twirling spaghetti

#474
Could you count
all of a shower's
raindrops?

#475
The jet's vapour trail
chalks a parabola
from west to east

#476
Holes poked in clouds
A sky giant's curious
fingers pressing

#477
After midnight's storm
cool fresh air
A wakeful stillness

#478
Darkest before dawn
they say – birds sing
their most urgent notes

#479
From my window
daybreak silhouettes –
sometimes, a shooting bird

#480
Before the sky lightens
birds hustle the day –
fresh voices old tunes

#481
This teething cat
chooses *Birds of Australia*
to chew – pulped parrots

#482
Crow with a twig
Renovated nest in
a flap or two

#483
Choosing the grass
footpath over concrete
Radical urban walking

#484
Two ibises pecking in
the park – mates or
pausing acquaintances?

#485
Crickets trill the same
long-note song
Telling shadow stories

#486
Worrying ahead of time
I fall behind
Stay here – now

#487
This morning's sky
borrowed from another
town's yesterday

#488
The rhythm of
a crow's wing-flap
building height – its hum

#489
That scooter's noise
far louder than its speed –
exhausting

#490
Currawongs and magpies
lawn-snacking
Working-class songbirds

#491 – *Daylight Saving Suite: 1*
From one minute
to the next
we lose an hour

#492 – *Daylight Saving Suite: 2*
Swapping morning
light for evening
Dark beginnings

#493 – *Daylight Saving Suite: 3*
Sun shining from
dawn to dusk
playing no favourites

#494 – *Daylight Saving Suite: 4*
Daylight saving even
on cloudy days
Summer's sleight of hand

#495 – *Daylight Saving Suite: 5*
Late afternoon
plenty of light
We squander it – ha!

#496 – *Daylight Saving Suite: 6*
Daylight saving ends
The hour returns
silently all at once

#497
Fog thins and thickens
the closer, the farther away
Over there, I disappear

#498
Fog descending
Planes rising
Temporary truce

#499
On my pale arms
the rising sun
attempting warmth

#500 – *Shadow Suite: 1*
Sunrise shadows stretch
and relax
A midday farewell

#501 – *Shadow Suite: 2*
Afternoon shade like
Nana's on Sunday
Biscuits and cordial, laughs

#502 – *Shadow Suite: 3*
Sunset shadows stretch
and disappear
Evening shift specialists

#503
A stand of trees
waiting for life
Still life still

#504
If a butterfly
sipped coffee would
it be a butterflatte?

#505
The drums next door
and rooftop rain
It must be Friday

#506
When more take the
road less travelled –
return to Main Street?

#507
Footpath showroom
New old furniture
tempting trawlersby

#508
Black white black white
Double decaff, latte light
Coffee drive-through

#509
A single raindrop
on my fingertip
The lightest shower

#510
My breath slowing
Stillness arriving
Tea cools

#511
Home-made biscuits
rough around the edges
Tasty, tastier

#512
Close your eyes
What did you see
before the blink?

#513
Man and puppy
walking the street
Trainer and 'A cat!'

#514
Girl and dog
running together the
frolic and the lollop

#515
Clouds like
fish skeletons
diving earthwards

#516
Little ibis
shorter beak
Leaning closer to breakfast

#517
The newest garden at
the newest house
Petals and paint preening

#518
Mother and skipping child
holding hands
One more tightly

#519
Cloudspread sky
Dabs streaks wrinkles
Airy fairy art

#520
Ground cover creeping
through the garden
Slo-mo takeover

#521
Fog thick like
meringue
the yolk unbeaten

#522
Clouds flattened
against the sky
like squashed gum

#523
Clouds pinched and pulled
by airy fingers
Sky wounds covered

#524
Circling the block
squaring the circle
Geometry of the walk

#525
Salmon and her
poaching pals:
butter lemon pepper

#526
The clumpiness of rice
starchy little grains
with attitude

#527
Tree stump smoothing
Black cat cruising
her new scratching post

#528
Pale blue plane
Pale blue sky
Disappearing act

#529
Crispy cool morning
days before Spring
Sun led petal-thaw

#530
This gathering-in of trees
a perspective illusion
They're streets apart

#531
Arriving at the bakery
for the last sourdough
A little burnt it is

#532
Can you walk the
wrong way along
a one-way street?

#533
Up down along
Who decides
these angles?

#534 – *Almost Died Life: #1*
At birth
umbilical cord choke hold
Doctor unlooping

#535 – *Almost Died Life: #2*
At six
gumball choking
Passing father's back slap

#536 – *Almost Died Life: #3*
At ten
the reversing drunk
Two steps early

#537
New suburban streets
pleating their way
uphill

#538
Street lamp
shift over
fades into dawn

#539
There's always
one more question
 What is it?

#540
Streets named after
battles remembered
for their names

#541
Begin on the minute
End on the hour
Walking time

#542
Begin in the moment
End in the moment
Present time

#543
Ball on the footpath
No kids apparent
Temptation steps up

#544
Each step
perfect
with attention

#545
Jasmine-scented tea
Breathe it sip
Lean close breathe

#546
On Heliopolis Parade
Walking cycling running driving
Suburban parade

#547
Two men
One boat
Captains both?

#548
Beachfront lunch
Gulls nipping
chips

#549
Foreshore ice-cream
Wind licking
drips

#550
Kids biking fast
faster breath-holding the
corners

#551
In life-changing moments
take a breath ...
take two

#552
Carrying the rain
with me
Umbrella drumming

#553
Spackle of round
fat drops
Windscreen wiping

#554
Bending the leaf
drop by drip
Waterfall tipping point

#555
Tree shelter silent
and dry as
showers boldly grow

#556
Watching the light
arrive, stealthy at
first, claiming shadows

#557 – *Food Court Suite: #1*
Sometimes a deep-fried
potato scallop hot
salty, crunchy, just one – ha!

#558 – *Food Court Suite: #2*
Pizza slice tomato
sausage stretchy cheese
an arm's length snap

#559 – *Food Court Suite: #3*
Burger and fries, drink
Bun-chew fry-bite
and sauce-dip, straw-sip

#560 – *Food Court Suite: #4*
Lamb salad tabouli
hommus, chilli sauce totally
wrapped in each other

#561
Flowers behind fences shaded
bird-nipped, mulched but
sun reaching, always

#562
At the new build
its' plasterers
prepare seamlessness

#563
Winter's tail
a Winter's tale
in Spring

#564
Leaves relieved of
their leafy tenure
join rakish gangs

#565
Chopper bisecting the
setting sun before
the horizon slice

#566
Plover ak-aking
Magpie larking
Tuneless worm turning

#567
Winter won't go
Summer won't stay
Springing hot and cold

#568
Tableless chairs on the
footpath the whole
set free

#569
Cloudless moonless
morning sky
painting the blues

#570
Jacaranda jacaranda
Oh, my
blooming jacaranda

#571
Little old lady, sun
hat tote bag hand
weights strong legs walking

#572
Clouds relaxing across
the dawn sky
before their day shift

#573
Bone-chilled on
a mild April night
A winter within

#574
Cinnamon nutmeg
jasmine scents, afternoon
tea plays Spring

#575
Noisy miner's
lowset nest
Downward-snapping beak

#576
Leaves blown
far from home
Groundlings abiding

#577
A feather glides in
to land no
longer winging it

#578
Crickets and geckoes
shushing and tutting
after the storm

#579
Yellow butterflies
ganging up on
the blue sky

#580
If toes could
speak would they
talk the walk?

#581
A snail crosses
my path slowly
slowly I wait

#582
Prints in dried mud
foot and paw
An earthed friendship

#583
New stairs for old
old feet wearing them
up and down

#584
Rainbow lorikeets in the
poinciana the more you
look the more you see

#585
Drops growing larger
I once caught a
shower this big.

#586
'Really?' I hear
from a passing car
Travelling incredulity

#587
Midnight lightning show
its' audience asleep
thunder claps for encores

#588
Outside my night
washed window the
silent light arrives

#589
In a new bed
do you dream
new dreams?

#590
Dawn's light
sluicing colour
through the streets

#591
Watching from photos
the ancestors' eyes
my eyes

#592
Silhouettes emerge
and leave
with dawn

#593
Sky-gazing childhood
searching for our
stardust parents

#594
On the corner
a vacant shop
leasing airy hope

#595
Soft growl half
bark feigning
mean-eyed threat

#596
A stretch of
carnations beyond gravity
The vase tilts

#597
The pregnant neighbour's
new garden growing
ahead of her

#598
Whipper-snipping
defenceless grass
Its' blades blunted

#599
A snake warms
itself nearby
ignoring my fear

#600
Blue car white van
red bike flagging
a breakfast baguette

#601
Garden shrubs lopped
and squared, precisely,
for a day

#602
Cup to kettle?
Kettle to cup?
Who cares? Pour.

#603
Clouds apprenticed to
the day
practice their colours and shapes

#604
The hoarder's neighbour
emptied one room
and danced in there

#605
Escapee beagle, legs
working, ears pinned
His owner the same

#606
Grey smudges on a
white-washed sky
The artist's palette shrinks

#607
Dawn's late-comers
shriek loudest
Their colours brighten

#608
Rock wall resting
with gravity in
stony silence

#609
The thickest summer
grass finds
its weekend feet

#610
Cement truck rolling
its' cargo to a
permanent stop

#611
Spiders, lizards, scurrying,
gliding things – abandoned
car eco-village

#612
A sweep of leaves
blown sideways
wheeling at the corner

#613
Only blue
as far as eyes can see
And beyond?

#614
Heat waving – and
laughing – its morning
to midnight mirth

#615
A hedge half trimmed
half wild
The garden's pentimento?

#616
Fountain grass
leaning for the
windiest gossip

#617
A hound howling
from suburban steps
His other steppe calling

#618
One smoke long:
the bus driver's wait
for his pick-up

#619
Oscar the Short's fence
no match for
Harriet the Tall

#620
At the sprinkler-face
weeds enjoy
randomized equality

#621
Car tracks on
a dusty road
Travelling conversation

#622
In my street I
step lively
Six houses to go

#623
Boy riding footpath
Too fast, I yell,
too loudly

#624
Smelling Sunday's roast
on Friday at
the rosemary bush

#625
Pinning her hair
before exams fearing
a let-down

#626
The chair's cushion
askew. Or the
cushion's chair?

#627
Chicken or eggs
for dinner?
Whichever cooks first

#628
The many-drawered
credenza and its
capacity for surprises

#629
Empty bottle full
minutes ago – my
thirst so strong?

#630
Mistaking the jet's fading
engine for thunder
Droughty illusions

#631
The cat's black
feather toy
Whose wing donated?

#632
Falling asleep on
the sofa just
the right length

#633
The comfort of
mild weather forgotten
until it's gone

#634
Sitting at the
window watching
the invisible wind show

#635
Grey clouds promising
rain before their
breezy farewell

#636
Mother and infant
exercise class these
babies fit for sleeping

#637
The builder's barking bulldog
greets me each day
with loving suspicion

#638
Old house removed
Old fence remains
binding airborne memories

#639
Wiggling my
shadow fingers tickling
the grass

#640
Zig-zagging among
fallen leaves waltzing
with eucalypt castoffs

#641
Losing my breath
at the hill's top
A searching descent

#642
The ginger cat
undisturbed in her
aged sleep

#643
Full moon bleaching the
night sky a lighter
shade of black

#644
Sister cats grooming
face wash by
paw lick

#645
Working after hours as
the garden's fairy
lights blink on

#646
My cat searches
for comfort on
a flat flat mat

#647
The slightest shift
of curtains – is the
heatwave breaking?

#648
Unknown runner on
a dark night street
Training, chasing, fleeing?

#649
One cat – too few
Three cats – too many
Two cats will do

#650
Tree hugging for
beginners: find an
arm-span's circumference

#651
Clumps of hail
corner the water
storage market, briefly

#652
News read
Soft drink drunk
Thought bubbles

#653
That scent of
lemon just turning
A squeeze left?

#654
Past a friend's house;
she's on holidays
A kind of absence

#655
Home as the
rain starts I
laugh at the sky

#656
April shower
in March
Instant gratification

#657
Beer can sweating
in the heat
losing its cool

#658
Where the water
main burst muddy
footprints sun-baking

#659
Pyramid of papers
after the holidays
Old news pressed

#660
Vacant lot vacant
for long enough
to air memories

#661
At year's end
fresh hope scorching
its way past midnight

#662
Storm-detecting cat
slinking down the hall
better than radar

#663
Breakfast the same
every day the
textures of familiars

#664
Rosemary bushes
fencing privacy
in

#665
Clouds comfort each
other pillow upon
cushion

#666
On moonless nights
even the raindrops
darkening

#667
New shop old
business its sign's
dusty past

#668
New shop old
business its sign
past dusting

#669
Sorting one drawer two
A cupboard's shelves
hosting emptiness

#670
Breezy gifts each
day from this
lemon-scented gum

#671
Old x-rays piled on
the top shelf
A bony jumble

#672
Fence palings following
each other following
falling fallen

#673
Folding clothes and
the day listening
to sunset's parrots

#674
Rain-addled trees
showering us with
stormy leftovers

#675
Sleepless in the
heatwave a night-scenting
jasmine for company

#676
Silence before a storm
as though there were
no more questions

#677
Greenery draping itself
over fences
Summer's casual hello

#678
One table two chairs
Standing room only
Tiny coffee shop

#679
Red carpet welcome as
I walk by
Man sweeping footpath

#680
Bamboo no match
for the gardener's blade
Regrowth matchless

#681
Building site cat scratching
almost-set footings
Secret house tattoo

#682
Empty bus stop seat
Mrs B___ deceased
Vacancy

#683
Brown bread cream
cheese yellow
mustard – beigey lunch

#684
Saturday afternoon scents on
Monday morning
Mower fuel grass vapours

#685
Write a poem write
it now write it oh
Wrong now

#686
Roads veined and cracking
Sideline trees and shrubs
rooting for nature

#687
Weeds, considered ugly,
grow happily anyway
towards the sun

#688
A distant kettle
boiling, a
tea cup nearby

#689
Waiting in line
my foot begins
its impatient tap

#690
Meeting old friends at
the usual place
iced coffee warm hearts

#691
Paper pile neatened
Calculator cooling
Taxing times behind

#692
Lauren Bacall-Cricket: *Just
put your wings
together and rub*

#693
A swoop of crows
hunting breakfast
cloaking the road

#694
At the library's herb
garden a summer of
leaves unbound

#695
Long-empty house
open to offers
hosts dust motes

#696
Old table on
the footpath memory
stained love-scratched

#697
Child-strewn swimming
pool, laughter
dripping everywhere

#698
Apple seeds on
the chopping board – no
place to grow

#699
The drip leaves
with
the plumber

#700
Bicycles pose
as sculptures
between rides

#701
The sunny street
art of fences
casting shady brushwork

#702
Veranda cats
stretchily resume
chairs for themselves

#703
Gutters running
like flat
waterfalls

#704
Dozens of paw-prints in
a rough circle
One dog – excited

#705
A storm arrives
after months we
sit and watch it blow

#706
Bees humming
a worker's tune
in honeyed solidarity

#707
Parrots on the
wing singing themselves
up to speed

#708
Piano practice
Dog barks baby cries
Everyone's a critic

#709
The gruffness of
thunder as though it
needs more attitude

#710
The sea breeze
from far off
reaches inland, whispering

#711
No politics today
or any other
would be a start

#712
An empty cup and
a bitey mosquito guide
my sunset retreat

#713
When it grows too dark
to write, find a star
and re-site, re-sight

#714
Dog strains his leash
Cat stands her ground
Barking and silence

#715
Shoe sole pebbles
barely fit the
profile

#716
Clothesline lost in
weeds – pegs clinging like
tiny birds, if you squint

#717
Take a number
Take a seat
Blood test queue

#718
A single feather
calming down to the
ground – weightless grace

#719
Lightning-struck tree regards
its sky horizontally –
a mild blue, now

#720
Chorus-line of
magpies branching out by
wing and warble

#721
Bananas bending over
backwards, or forwards,
to fit in

#722
An embarrassment of
apples, the redder
the better

#723
Garlic oil running
rings around onion, the
scent of competition

#724
Celery and cucumber
stalking and envious vegetables
before their salad days

#725
Bell pepper kebab
Red yellow green
Nightshade traffic lights

#726
Reading one novel
all day an
other-worldly Saturday

#727
Out with threatening clouds
at my usual pace
Who's bluffing?

#728
After fasting
beginner's palate the
tastiness of – anything

#729
The gardener, head
bowed, pays
her digging homage

#730
Gliding magpies
mother and fledglings
A cappella trio

#731
Cloud in from
the sea full of
rainy news

#732
At the unkempt hedge
a wild longing
for symmetry

#733
A lost cup down
on its luck and its side
Saucerless and empty

#734
Leaves where they
should be
Treed, and strewn

#735
Sprinkling water
after the drought
A grassy benediction

#736
Rare teddy bears
boxed and shelved
Safety love

#737
In the healthiest garden
resistance writes and rises
There is munching

#738
Is an empty
room the
tidiest?

#739
The mild first of
autumn her seasonal fans
stretch and breathe, mildly

#740
At the army base
practice fire
Which enemy today?

#741
Black cat and
a black and white bird
Magpie and the flightless

#742
Socks unpaired in
the wash granted
autonomy down the line

#743
Table bump
Tea spill
Brimful no more

#744
A single traffic
cone upstandingly orange
protecting a black hole

#745
Woman with walking
stick almost jogging
Fastish-track rehab.

#746
Ants and crows at
the street scrap diner
Pop-up shop

#747
A petal falls
behind the fence
shyly letting go

#748
The sorrowful dog
barks an apology
for barking

#749
Cords of poles on
rows of trucks
Linear friends

#750
At table's end
my cat dozes
Her ears don't

#751
In early sun the
garden shimmies to a
silent dance tune breeze

#752
Prowling the kitchen
with a cheetah's gait
our slimmer cat snacking

#753
Apple and banana
sliced into friendship
over breakfast

#754
The moving van
half full
Coming or going?

#755
Baby with a blank
slate her hands
full of colours

#756
The sound of
one hand clapping
may be breezy

#757
Mother with straggling
child – she waits
he grows

#758
Down the grate
my faithful pen its
inky depths unwritten

#759
In the darkness rain
sounds like steam
hissing up a storm

#760
The old lady who walks
every day
Her new umbrella – red

#761
Rowing a straight line
through curling curving surf
The water's playfulness

#762
At the garage sale
strolling chickens
Priceless pats free

#763
Tripping not falling
at the corner's turn a
balance appreciation class

#764
Anxious to appear calm
she sketches the waiting room
and erases it

#765
Leashless dog smiling
as he bounds closer
nuzzles my wary palm

#766
Follow the stretching
cat's layabout lead
on Sunday, anyway

#767
Empty laundry basket
beneath the line
fills with shadow clothes

#768
Tea half drunk
Toast half eaten
Emergency? Distraction? Overslept.

#769
Looking right and left
on an empty street
belt and braces habit

#770
Perfectly perpendicular towers
founded in river rock
and geometry

#771
On the fridge
old magnets hold
new reminders

#772
Cheese tomato cucumber
carrot Himalayan pink salt
sprinkled from a height

#773
Bananas draped over
apples in the bowl
Lumpy red mattresses

#774 – *Rushing Suite #1*
The nurse rushing
to draw blood
the patient's pulse quickens

#775 – *Rushing Suite #2*
The muse rushing
to mix colours the
artist's palette knife hovers

#776 – *Rushing Suite #3*
The muse rushing
to whisper words
the writer's hands flexed

#777
Utensils hanging from
their kitchen rail
always at attention

#778
Post leaning
against tree
remembering earthier times

#779
Past my house
as though I'm a stranger
Who lives there?

#780
Soda water bubble pops
at my cat's nose
Is it salty?

#781
'Citrus' the word
sounds more lemony
than lemon

#782
Junk mail at the
empty house
unaddressed unread

#783
Dogs greeting each
other like old
puppy school friends

#784
Wind through trees
reminding them who's boss
The resistance rustles

#785
My shadow and
her sunny disposition
whatever my mood

#786
Walking by the
bees so closely honey
and toast breakfast

#787
Mother running
Child biking
Breathlessly together

#788
Late for work again
Breakfast on the trot
with cereal offenders

#789
Newly laid turf
in ill-fitting squares
An awkward adolescence

#790
Playground roundabout
primed by wind
spinning for ghosts

#791
The indecisive walker
North west south east?
chooses tea – and scones – jam

#792
Toasted ham and cheese sandwich
with chips
And tea – for health

#793
Before the construction
crew the deconstruction gang
They look alike

#794
A stormfront hurrying
to deadline, gusts
ahead of itself

#795
Fallen leaves rising
as hedgerows their
colourless history

#796
Autumn day pretending
it's Summer – our drinks
sweat and warm

#797
Hasten slowly every day
that could be
our last, or first

#798
Three pink blooms in
a white-blooming garden
Soft defiance

#799
Tall parents
Short child he
runs they walk

#800
In drought
the merest hint
of a specky drop, noted

#801
School bus
and children
idling before the bell

#802
Children running, laughing
and shouting their
morning laps

#803
Footprints in concrete
outgrown
by Summer's end

#804
DOT50's number plate
pinning her in
time, and model

#805
Noisy miners
beak-snap swooping snooping
crows

#806
The man who
ran with two
dogs, now one

#807
A sander
sounding angry
beautifying floors

#808
Mismatched fence palings
painted unpainted narrow wide
do the job

#809
Stray hubcap leans
against a tree
casually lost

#810
Taking the low road
shaded by the high
a Summer treat

#811
Walking mindfully
with each step?
No worries

#812
Worshipping the traffic light
trinity at intervals
Otherwise agnostic

#813
Newly turned soil its
very old memories
scent the air

#814
Storm clouds bridging
blue gaps
Sky engineers

#815
After the road-sweeper
a single stone left
Suddenly precious

#816
At the build
flowers grow
challenging concrete

#817
A young tree growing
shade for any passersby
Democracy in action

#818
After the storm
the muddy park
child attractant

#819
When it's sunless, clouds
glare at us instead
Pale imitations

#820
Trees sag
leaves droop the weight
of watery evidence

#821
Beneath the city's foggy
shroud its most
innocent undercover work

#822
Carrying an umbrella
all day while
the sun decides

#823
Cornflakes and milk better
with honey better
with tea better crunchy

#824
The buns we like
no longer sold
'They' didn't tell us

#825
The ladder that fell
resting comfortably
No head for heights

#826
From the sunny
to the shady
side light relief

#827
Barking from both
sides a street
of welcome

#828
A hunger of road
workers on our quiet
street silently lunching

#829
So slim it slides
between door and
floor an unassuming light

#830
Jumping dogs wagging
at each other
Leash-shortened friendship

#831
Two plovers legging
it as though they've
forgotten their wings

#832
The leash changing hands
Their favourite shared
The favoured leads them on

#833
A thoroughly emptied
passionfruit a
thoroughly filled possum

#834
The bush turkey
strafed by Noisy
Miners simply ambles

#835
After the storm
a garden conference
We Will Rebloom

#836
Trees market
the wind
noising it up

#837
After the fast
After the scan
Scanning fast food

#838
Cigarette smoke from
a passing car
scenting another's passing

#839
Storm-cleaned air not
making hay fever
while the sun shines

#840
Red rooves darkening
Their mouldy adventures
mapped tile by tile

#841
The flood tide
rises slowly a
low rolling spread

#842
The flood river's
silt tidily left
in furrowed layers

#843
A fledgling flood tops
the river's banks
and trickles at first

#844
The slow flood
patiently rising to
meet important customers

#845
Broken glass reflecting
sunny highlights
A useful beauty

#846
One tree after
another spruiking shade even
on sunless days

#847
My pen tip
still eager to
write, though inkless

#848
Perennial heat and
seasonal blindness the
comfort of tea

#849
Grate glaze ribbon
roast steam slice
boil – carrot carnival

#850
The pruned tree
hiding nothing but
its shadowy past

#851
Rendering walls to
the radio's Top 40
the textures swirl

#852
Dewfall settles on
grass and bird
Blade-slump and feather-shake

#853
A snail's pace at
full pelt, blink
and you'll see it

#854
A plover pair
walking the park imagine
them holding wings

#855
Stone spray as
the car corners gravel
rashing the road

#856
My brother singing
tears from Mum when
he was four

#857
Silence in the
neighbourhood,
the familiar we ignore

#858
Already the two-day-vacant
lot is feeding
birds and welcomes cats

#859
My hat brim grazes
a drooping frond
Stowaway lady bug

#860
The Weimaraner puppy
all legs and ears
on the loose

#861
Walking the beach
home with sand
in my shoes

#862
Trowel in hand
the amateur bricklayer
imagines a tea break

#863
The curved branch
bowing in reverence
to its roots

#864
Drought river in
flood jogging its'
memory to run

#865
One last drop
of moon to fill
its' lunar circle

#866
A crow bigger
than my cat within
cuddling distance – no

#867
Traffic building tiny
mobile homes every
morning at six

#868
Children's footsteps upstairs
The children grown and gone
Their echoes reminisce

#869
Beneath the shade
of breaking waves
water-cooled air

#870
The poinciana
bowing low
for a pat

#871
Fallen headstone
facing earth
Gravity's time-worn hostage

#872
Cappacino Cuppachino
Capuchino Coppachino
Coffee and frothy milk

#873
'Mmm,' I reply to
the barking dog
We have an understanding

#874
Leaf shadows playing
wall games on
a sunny day

#875
Beside the shiny
new an elderly
bike, gearing down

#876
The tall eucalypt felled
Leaves bleeding oil
scenting its death

#877
'Shoes on?' asks
the Dad. 'Soon,'
the boy replies.

#878
New puppies on the bark
running the yard
delight in their tails

#879
A double rainbow as
the sun appears
One each, my love

#880
This greenless, treeless
yard hoping for
a personality transplant

#881
Tiny poem in
a towering world tiny
from space

#882
Walking through a
sun-struck spider-thread
my cheek tickles

#883
Leaves rolling beside
me blow ahead to
welcome me home

#884
Clouds like thread-pulled
cotton waiting
for the iron

#885
Leafy confetti from
the poinciana
Small world celebration

#886
The upturned hat
welcoming sunshine
beneath its' brim

#887
Paw and fang
Claw and beak
Cat and crow tearing paper

#888
Solo sky dabs
join each other in
a stormy chorus

#889
A leaf falling
for gravity
the old romantic

#890
Sharpened tools inside
the shiny shed
for the dullest jobs

#891
Only my steps
in midnight's street
until I stop

#892
A slow bee
buzzing bottlebrush tired
of spreading gossip

#893
That tree full of
lorikeets, screeching
fans of dawn

#894
A tractor gang at
the vacant lot
shaking down the soil

#895
The sun rising
behind cloudy steps
in momentary shyness

#896
The kind of dog who
could wear a Homberg
and carry a violin case

#897
On the playing field
rehearsing for work
the children sweat

#898
The mystery bird
and its' daily song
Invisible familiar

#899
The old house in
new hands its
timbers creak a shiver

#900
Short sleeves sunscreen sweat
salad iced tea ice-cream
Autumn's Summer fling

#901
The single graffito tag
on the long pale fence
a signature threat

#902
The fairy lights blink
off at dawn
for a sunny holiday

#903
Pass the past
books into the present
for future reference

#904
In the orangesphere
sweetness and bite
and elegant quarters

#905
I ask the gardener
her tree's name
'Cynthia,' she says.

#906
Cracks in the pavement
Blue vein legs
We both manage

#907
Some days coarse
Other days silken with
these textured cats

#908
My billions of atoms
billions of years old
Where's the wisdom?

#909
The ibis, large and
beaky, flaps off
with languid gravitas

#910
Winter's cat
huddled on my lap
Smaller by degrees

#911
The merest misty
sprinkle dries with
each wing-flap

#912
Wind rippling
flat water in
breezy conversation

#913
Table salt
all over
the table

#914
Peppercorns cracked
and broken-in
for dinner

#915
Raindrops left after
the storm free-fall
without notice

#916
A raindrop hits
my fingertip
The tiniest splash

#917
After hospital blue
sky still blue
still

#918
Sketchy clouds tickling
the sky stretching
their wispy luck

#919
In the yellow
banksia rainbow lorikeets
colour-bombing

#920
Kids perkier, dogs
barkier, breakfast tastier
on the weekend

#921
Sunday bees and
Monday bees
sweetly toiling

#922
Coat hanger on
the fence
Outdoor clothing line

#923
Monday's dawn fog-burn
from
mind and sky

#924
Boris and Bradley
puppies at large
Next is what's next

#925
A new marigold
garden from my old
neighbour sowing Spring

#926
The part-time build
and its new roof
That cosy pride

#927
Fun runners seriously
checking their times, it's
everything, funnily enough

#928
The delicate lapping
of a cat's tongue
Pink ripple

#929
The shapeliness of
leaf-shadow its
mid-morning sway

#930
A round brown dog
resting as heavily as
a wet carpet roll

#931
In dogland one
unfamiliar footstep
is growl-worthy

#932
Reading through hours
page by chapter a
time-word continuum

#933
A dead worm
attended by ants
appears millipedal

#934
Broken mower
on the footpath
Grass heckling

#935
Swapping shoe for slipper
after work, stepping
into the sweet spot

#936
The imperfection of
Saturday afternoon
without a casual sleep

#937 – *Shady Duet #1*
Driving through
shadow lines
Momentary racing stripes

#938 – *Shady Duet #2*
Walking beneath
line shadow
A temporary tattoo

#939
Beneath the umbrella and
beneath the shady tree
Double cool

#940
A fallen branch stacked
with its brothers and sisters
in veteran silence

#941
A late in the
day sun-shower with
minutes to spare

#942
The crow tempted
by roadkill navigates
rain and wheels

#943
Shaken by gustiness
some leaves appear
frightened – others, drunk

#944
Reluctant dog at
the new vet's door
Can he read?

#945
Stepping between raindrops
while the clouds
decide – now? or there?

#946
Yearning for the
irretrievable I stare
down my mirrored self

#947
A cat at either
end and, in between,
the rug's playing field

#948
Windows rattle glassy-eyed
greetings to a chopper
flying far too low

#949
I make my mother's
pikelets, though there
are better recipes

#950
A small black spider
alights upon my keyboard
jittering its lettered dance

#951
The smell of blue
ink drying
in wordy silence

#952
Sunday night's rain
dripping past midnight down
Monday's slippery slope

#953
The cat nudges my
foot my foot nudges back
we settle

#954
When all is lost
or so it seems, write
the dark night to dawn

#955
Two Little Corellas intent
on their breakfast tree
ignore my hungry lens

#956
What is my cat
thinking, her paw
in mid-lift, so still

#957
Three chairs at angles
missing their fourth, make
do at the table

#958
Stand at the door
of an empty room
Your absence

#959
This wall of books
my reading life
foxed earmarked underlined

#960
Rainbow lorikeets flocking
in the red bottlebrush
That party screech

#961
The rain
thrilling across tin rooves
hears itself laugh

#962
There are only so
many years left I
dilly-dally all the same

#963
The new sofa welcoming
its first sleeper
relaxes just a little

#964
Throughout the house are
pairs of cheap glasses
to read expensive books

#965
On my grandmother's
birthday coincidental fireworks
We appropriate them

#966
Blooming ant hills with
the rain – mini volcanoes
already extinct

#967
There is rain that
falls like an afterthought
from clearing skies

#968
Our photo albums stacked
upon each other countless
faces cheek to cheek

#969
Three chess sets
in one room
I play Scrabble

#970
Waiting for inky
words to dry and
set in paper

#971
The smell of roast chicken
on salad night
Envy on the breeze

#972
The neighbour is selling
his car he washes
it, just this once

#973
Yesterday's news and
today's, page-bound
paper-set, persistent

#974
Digging post-holes
Turning old soil
to face the sun

#975
Fence palings pale
into yesterday's garden
paying the sun's toll

#976
Inside the photograph
we notice
no edges

#977
Summer's cat-shed
rolling with fan breeze
Chaotic fur mice

#978
Counting sheep to
sleep; which one
will it be?

#979
Hands relaxing after work
embrace each other
Familiar, warm

#980
Our neighbour asleep,
his TV wide awake
Us, too.

#981
In the black sky
night a quarter moonful
of brightening light

#982
At her funeral
wondering between hymns
whose turn is next

#983
Heat waving
summer off towards
autumn's tepid welcome

#984
Running uphill on the
field of dreams its
grass a smoother mat

#985
Midnight cough at a
distant house – flu
season an autumn away

#986
A sketchy shower
on a wispy breeze
It's late let's sleep

#987
The burnt night sky
after lightning strikes
sewing heaven and earth

#988
Warm legs
Cold arms
Half baked

#989
Sirens and babies wailing
Dogs and cats misbehaving
Full moon

#990
There is always room
for more relaxation
Go ahead and spread

#991
The good moon
rising surely slowly
How lovely to sleep

#992
Midday heat at
midnight even the
stars are sweating

#993
Despite everything
in some moments
there is peace

#994
One drip per breath
then two three more
The parsimonious shower

#995
The wind-blown newspaper
of sad bad stories
tears around the block

#996
Humidity lifts like
old wallpaper slowly
reluctantly in a swelter

#997
Talking to yourself?
Slow down, take
your time, relax

#998
Sometimes I dream symphonies
and artworks. They're
real. They're gone.

#999
What earthly things will
you miss? Rain and grass,
the breeze. My ocean

#1000
Crows bully us awake
Magpies sing
us to dreams

Acknowledgements

Thank you to those with whom I've been lucky enough to share moments of love, kindness and support in this life and, sometimes, well, often, sheer joy, silliness, and comic relief. We are all poor pilgrims on a mystery tour. Who knows where it ends or what we'll find, but one thing is certain: there's no point in worrying about it, though of course, we will.

Thanks, and love to, among others (alphabetically, what could be fairer): Adam S, Andrea S, Brendan C, Callie, Carol M, Dash, Dorothy (Dot) P, Dotty (Donut), Emma H, Estelle P, Hayley H, Helen B, Jan McK, Jodi B, John McL, Julie C, Kym S, Leone H, Mottle (Momo), Noel G, Suzanne L, Wayne F.

Whomever I've forgotten (sorry), put it down to far too much youthful boozing and far too many anaesthetics.

But always, and always, Lorrie.

About the Author

Jay Verney is an Australian writer who has published in a range of genres. She lives in Queensland with her partner, Lorrie, and enjoys baking bread and cakes, and making pizza. She enjoys eating and sharing those things even more. She would have liked to have been a disciplined, ascetic kind of person, but alas, those traits eluded her. Jay also has two cats who are quite lovely. Thank you for reading.